DISCOVERING
PLANETS & MOONS

Kelly Gauthier

APPLESAUCE PRESS

KENNEBUNKPORT, MAINE

13-Digit ISBN: 9781604338003
10-Digit ISBN: 1604338008

This book may be ordered by mail from the publisher. Please include $5.99 for postage and handling.
Please support your local bookseller first!

Books published by Cider Mill Press Book Publishers are available at special discounts for bulk purchases in the United States by corporations, institutions, and other organizations.
For more information, please contact the publisher.

Applesauce Press is an imprint of
Cider Mill Press Book Publishers
"Where good books are ready for press"
PO Box 454
12 Spring Street
Kennebunkport, Maine 04046

Visit us online! cidermillpress.com

Typography: Gipsiero, Destroy, Imperfect, PMN Caecilia
Images used under license from Getty Images: pages 38 (Universal History Archive / #:179799087) and 72 (Bettmann / #:517359840); page 66 ESO/L. Calçada and Nick Risinger (skysurvey.org); page 71 Courtesy NASA/JPL-Caltech

All other images used under official license from Shutterstock.com

Printed in China

2 3 4 5 6 7 8 9 0

TABLE OF CONTENTS

INTRODUCTION 5

PLANETS 8

MOONS 24

GALAXIES 42

STARS 50

DWARF PLANETS 60

SPACE TECHNOLOGY 68

SUPERLATIVES 76

INDEX 84

The Earth and Sun, as seen from space.

INTRODUCTION

It's hard to imagine what is beyond our planet, but in reality, the universe is much bigger than life on Earth.

Looking up at the sky can tell us a lot about the universe, and ancient astronomers did just that as they started exploring space. During the day, the Sun and clouds show just a hint of what's beyond Earth... but at night the Moon and stars show us that there is far more out there than first meets the eye.

The invention of the telescope in the early 1600s gave us a new way to look at the sky. Astronomers could see much farther into space—far beyond what merely their eyes could see. They mapped and calculated, and spent years trying to learn more about space.

In the 1960s, we made another huge stride in space exploration by sending humans into outer space! To investigate what lies beyond our world, humans have studied the Moon and stars from spaceships, walked on the Moon, and even lived in outer space in the International Space Station (page 73).

WHAT IS IN SPACE?

Once you leave planet Earth, there is no breathable air in the atmosphere. That's why astronauts have to wear large oxygen tanks when they are outside of their spaceship.

Outer space is black, but that doesn't mean it's empty. Gas, dust, and matter make up most of space, but there are also objects like planets (page 9), moons (page 25), galaxies (page 43), stars (page 51), and dwarf planets (page 61). There are also smaller objects like meteors, asteroids, and comets that move throughout space.

Two interesting elements of space are supernovas and black holes. When a star runs out of fuel, it explodes; this explosion forms a supernova. Black holes are areas where nothing—not even light—can escape from. These mysteries of space are hard to understand because scientists have not been able to explore them.

Objects in space are not stationary; most travel in an orbit around another object. Sometimes, these moving objects collide.

It's impossible for us to measure the size and age of space. Our explorations have led us to find objects that are billions of years old. Distance in space is measured in light years, or the distance that light travels in one year.

Despite all of our explorations, we have not yet found evidence of other forms of life in space.

Humans are explorers by nature, and that desire to explore extends far beyond the boundaries of Earth. But our own curiosity is not the only reason to care about what happens in space.

Our lives are ruled by the Sun and Moon; the Sun's rays heat our planet, the Moon's gravity controls the ocean's tides, and together they set our days and nights. Also important is the fact that other objects in space are not stationary and are constantly moving around our planet; understanding the objects in the universe and their location helps us to better understand our own planet.

Although we have not yet found evidence of life on other planets, scientists hope to determine if there are other planets that could support life. This doesn't just mean looking for aliens. It means that scientists are looking for planets with appropriate temperatures, a stable atmosphere, and sufficient water; together, these three things would allow plants or people to grow and thrive. As of now, humans could not live on any other planet, but scientists are always looking to see whether it would be possible.

Space is made up of matter and elements, many of which are also present on Earth. In our own ever-changing climate, however, it is important for us to understand the different matter and forces in the universe that could have the potential to give us new forms of energy.

Our Sun (center) and its solar system, from left to right: Pluto (a dwarf planet), Neptune, Uranus, Saturn, Jupiter, Mars, Earth, Venus, and Mercury.

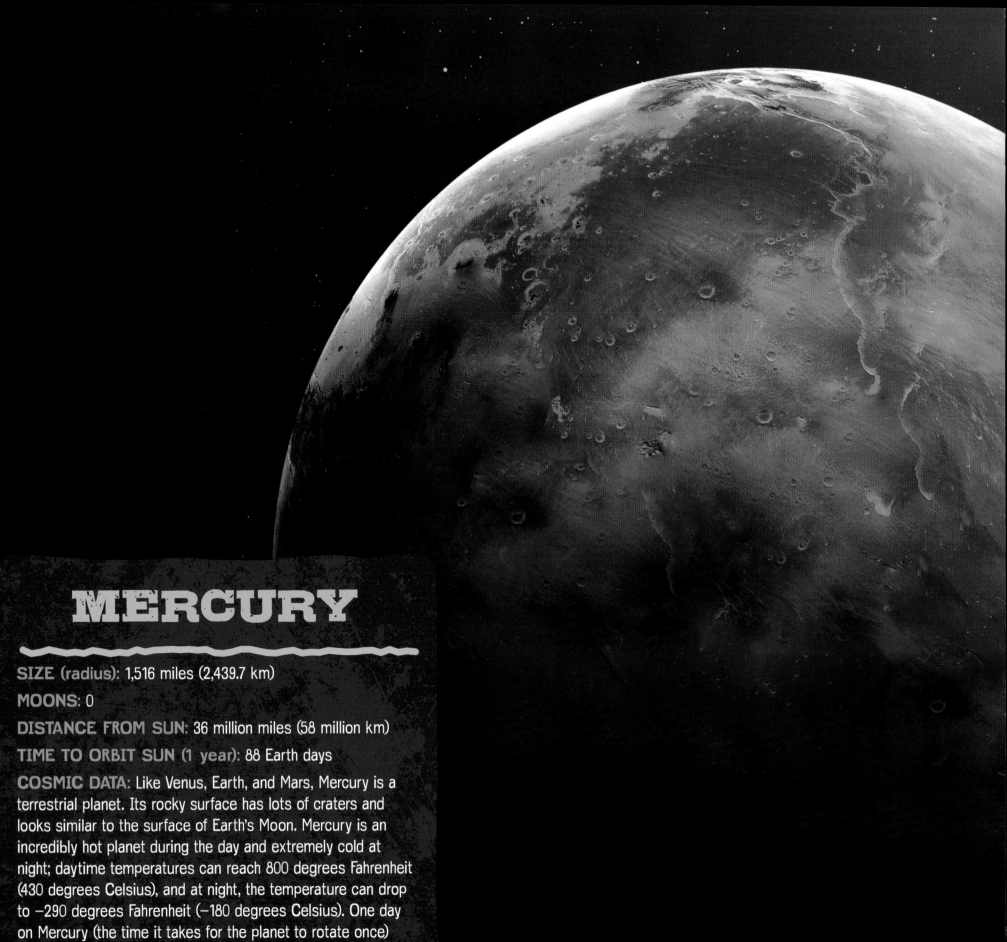

MERCURY

SIZE (radius): 1,516 miles (2,439.7 km)

MOONS: 0

DISTANCE FROM SUN: 36 million miles (58 million km)

TIME TO ORBIT SUN (1 year): 88 Earth days

COSMIC DATA: Like Venus, Earth, and Mars, Mercury is a terrestrial planet. Its rocky surface has lots of craters and looks similar to the surface of Earth's Moon. Mercury is an incredibly hot planet during the day and extremely cold at night; daytime temperatures can reach 800 degrees Fahrenheit (430 degrees Celsius), and at night, the temperature can drop to −290 degrees Fahrenheit (−180 degrees Celsius). One day on Mercury (the time it takes for the planet to rotate once)

PLANETS

According to the International Astronomical Union, in order for an object in space to be considered a planet, it must orbit a sun, but it cannot be a moon of another space object. A planet must also be round, and large enough to move objects (such as asteroids and comets) out of its way to continue its orbit. Because of the last reason, Pluto—formerly considered a planet—was renamed to the dwarf planet category in 2006.

Our solar system has eight objects that are officially classified as planets, and are typically ordered by how far away they are from the Sun: Mercury, Venus, Earth, Mars, Jupiter, Saturn, Uranus, and Neptune.

There are three different types of planets in our solar system: terrestrial, gas giant, and ice giant. The first four planets from the Sun—Mercury, Venus, Earth, and Mars—are terrestrial planets. This type of planet has a rocky, solid surface. The next two planets—Jupiter and Saturn—are gas giant planets. The opposite of terrestrial planets, the gas giant planets are mostly made up of gas. The last two planets—Uranus and Neptune—are ice giant planets because they are primarily made up of ice.

Mercury is the smallest of the eight planets and is closest to our Sun.

VENUS

SIZE (radius): 3,760 miles (6,052 km)

MOONS: 0

DISTANCE FROM SUN: 67 million miles (108 million km)

TIME TO ORBIT SUN (1 year): 225 Earth days

COSMIC DATA: Unlike most of the other planets, Venus rotates backward, so the Sun rises in the west and sets in the east. One day on Venus (the time it takes for the planet to rotate once) takes about 243 Earth days because of this backward rotation. Like Mercury, Mars, and Earth, Venus is a terrestrial planet, but its surface is unique because it has many volcanoes—far more than on Earth. Venus also has winds that blow with the force of a hurricane, and has been visited by more than 40 spacecraft.

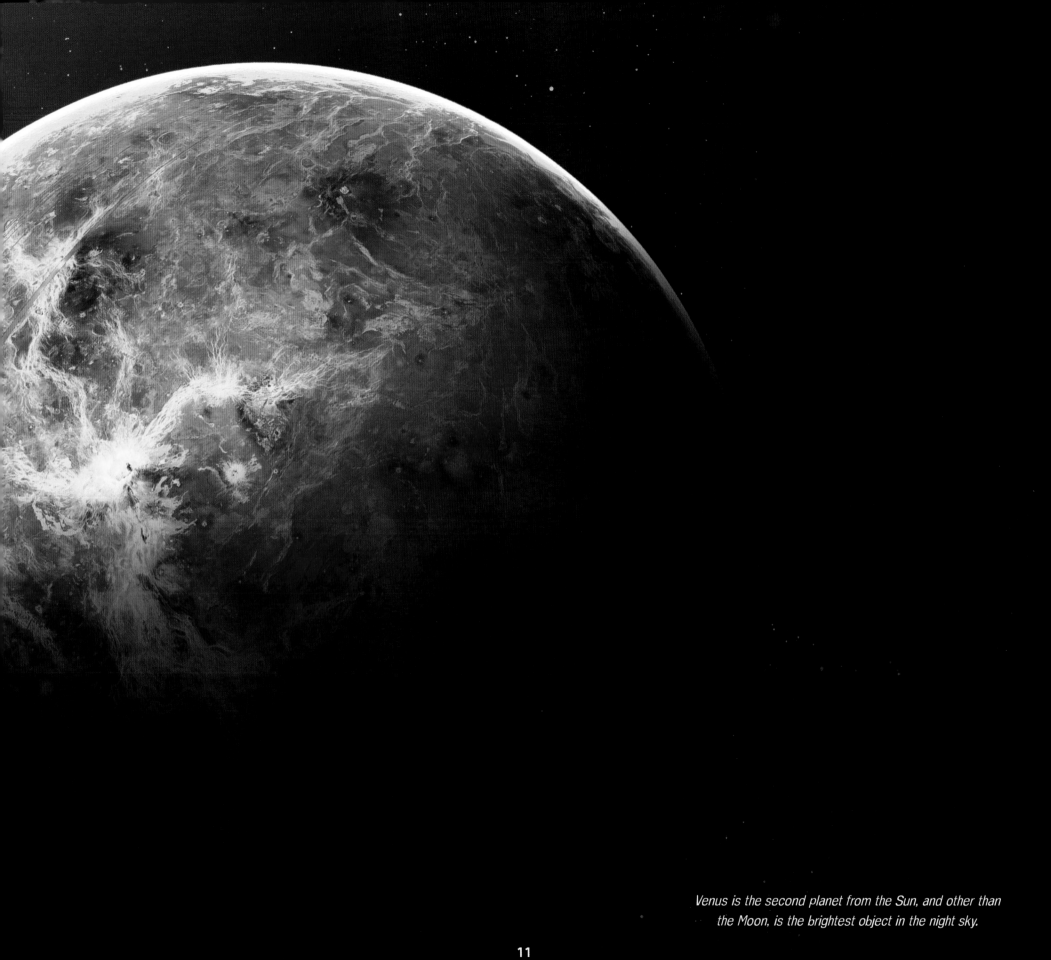

Venus is the second planet from the Sun, and other than the Moon, is the brightest object in the night sky.

EARTH

SIZE (radius): 3,959 miles (6,371 km)

MOONS: 1

DISTANCE FROM THE SUN: 93 million miles (150 million km)

TIME TO ORBIT SUN (1 year): 365 days

COSMIC DATA: Like Mercury, Venus, and Mars, Earth is a terrestrial planet. While the surface of our home planet has canyons, plains, and mountains, it is mostly covered in water. Earth is the only life-supporting planet within our solar system; the atmosphere here is mostly nitrogen and oxygen, which both allows us to breathe and protects the Earth from any incoming meteors or asteroids. Earth is also the only planet with one moon. Astronauts have spent a long time studying our Moon and viewing Earth from space.

Supplied by NASA, this is an image of planet Earth as it appears from space; the bright areas are lights from densely populated areas.

Mars is a desolate terrestrial planet;
the white area is a permanent polar ice cap.

MARS

SIZE (radius): 2,106 miles (3,390 km)

MOONS: 2

DISTANCE FROM SUN: 142 million miles (228 million km)

TIME TO ORBIT SUN (1 year): 687 Earth days

COSMIC DATA: Like Mercury, Venus, and Earth, Mars is a terrestrial planet with a very rocky surface. Mars has been nicknamed the Red Planet, because the minerals that make up its surface have a distinctive rusty color. Mars has two moons, Phobos (page 28) and Deimos. Mars has a similar day length to Earth, with one rotation taking about 24 hours, but—because it is farther away from the Sun—a year on Mars is almost double the length of a year on Earth. Currently, scientists have found no evidence of life on Mars, but there are ongoing space missions to help us decide whether the planet could support life.

JUPITER

SIZE (radius): 43,440.7 miles (69,911 km)

MOONS: 53 confirmed, 16 provisional

DISTANCE FROM SUN: 484 million miles (778 million km)

TIME TO ORBIT SUN (1 year): 12 Earth years

COSMIC DATA: The first of the gas giant planets, Jupiter is similar to a star because it was formed from swirling gas. Unlike the terrestrial planets, Jupiter does not have a truly solid surface. Scientists suggest that there may be a solid core, but this has not been confirmed. Jupiter, which is surrounded by rings, has at least 53 orbiting moons, as well as the shortest day in our solar system—less than 10 hours long. There is an area on Jupiter called the Great Red Spot—a giant storm that has been active for more than a century.

Jupiter is the largest planet in our solar system; in this image, you can clearly see the Great Red Spot!

Scientists at NASA believe the ice and rocks contained in Saturn's rings could be pieces of comets, asteroids, or moons that were torn apart by the planet's powerful gravity.

SATURN

SIZE (radius): 36,183.7 miles (58,232 km)

MOONS: 53 confirmed, 9 provisional

DISTANCE FROM SUN: 886 million miles (1.4 billion km)

TIME TO ORBIT SUN (1 year): 29 Earth years

COSMIC DATA: Saturn is the farthest planet from Earth to be discovered without a telescope, and it was named for a Roman god. Like Jupiter, Saturn is a gas giant and is made of swirling gas, so it does not have a solid surface. A day on Saturn is just 10.7 hours long—only slightly longer than Jupiter's day. Saturn has seven distinct rings made up of chunks of ice and rocks. The *Cassini* spacecraft was sent to investigate Saturn, and its mission ended when it was destroyed in the planet's atmosphere...which probably means that there's debris from *Cassini* orbiting Saturn!

19

Uranus is the seventh planet from the Sun and has 27 known natural satellites (moons).

URANUS

SIZE (radius): 15,759.2 miles (25,362 km)

MOONS: 27

DISTANCE FROM SUN: 1.8 billion miles (2.9 billion km)

TIME TO ORBIT SUN (1 year): 84 Earth years

COSMIC DATA: Uranus is the first of the ice giants, and most of the planet is made up of icy material around a solid core. Uranus was the first planet discovered by using a telescope, and only one spacecraft (*Voyager 2*, page 68) has ever flown by the planet. Uranus has 13 rings around it, as well as 27 moons—and each moon is named after a character created by the writers William Shakespeare and Alexander Pope. Like Venus, Uranus rotates backward, but Uranus is unique because it rotates on its side.

NEPTUNE

SIZE (radius): 15,299.4 miles (24,622 km)

MOONS: 13 confirmed, 1 provisional

DISTANCE FROM SUN: 2.8 billion miles (4.5 billion km)

TIME TO ORBIT SUN (1 year): 165 Earth years

COSMIC DATA: Neptune, the other ice giant, is farthest from the Sun in our solar system, and like Uranus, is made up of icy material around a small core. Neptune is known for being the windiest planet in the solar system. It has 5 known rings and 13 moons, and each moon is named after a god or nymph from mythology. The dwarf planet Pluto is usually farther away from the Sun than Neptune, but Pluto has a strange orbit path that sometimes brings it closer to the Sun than Neptune.

Neptune is the farthest planet from the Sun; until its redesignation as a dwarf planet, Pluto held this title.

Earth's Moon—our planet's only permanent, natural satellite.

MOONS

Look up into the sky at night and you can usually see Earth's Moon.

A lot of the planets have several moons around them, and some have many. Astronomers started discovering moons in the 1600s and were surprised to learn that planets other than Earth had them.

Moons are objects in space that naturally orbit around a particular planet. Even dwarf planets can have moons. A variety of different things can be found on a moon's surface—ice, mountains, craters...even volcanoes!

Even though scientists estimate that there are at least 181 moons in our solar system, humans have only set foot on one: Earth's Moon.

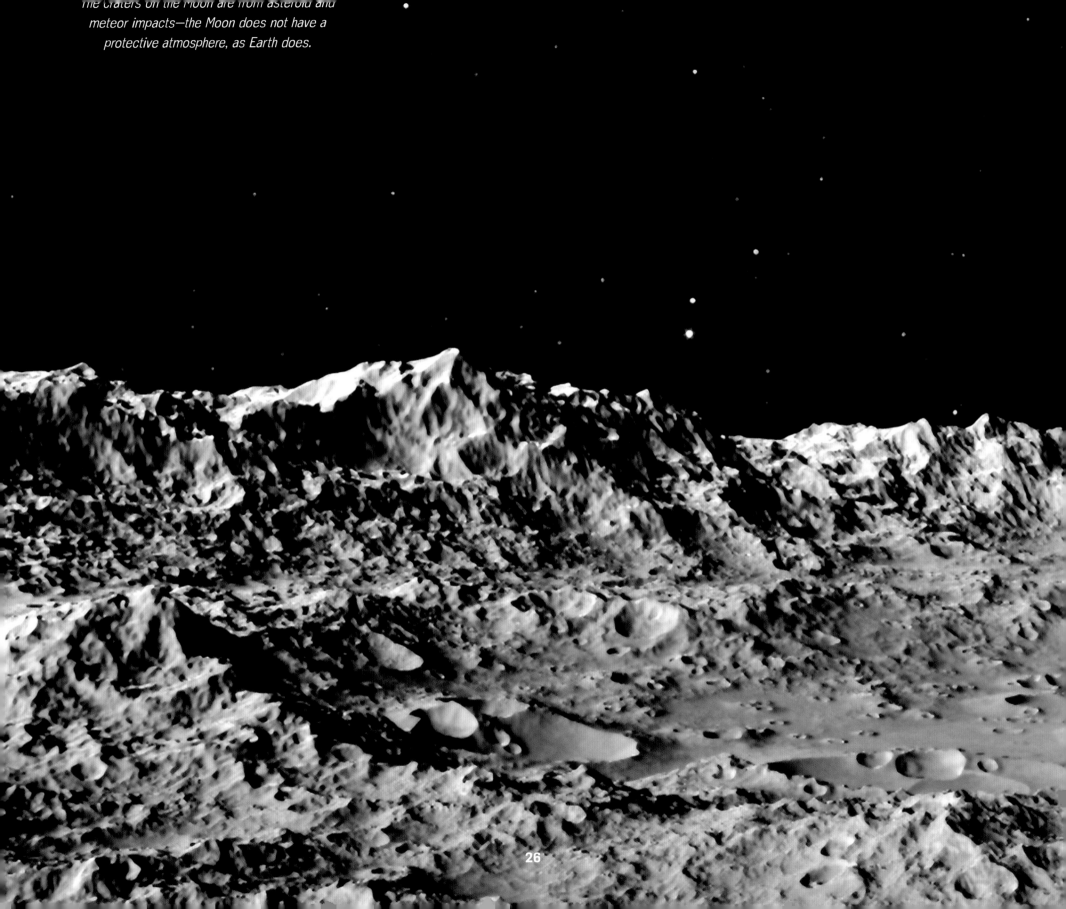

The craters on the Moon are from asteroid and meteor impacts—the Moon does not have a protective atmosphere, as Earth does.

EARTH'S MOON

SIZE (diameter): 2,159 miles (3,474.6 km)

PLANET IT ORBITS: Earth (page 12)

DISCOVERED: Unknown

NAMED FOR: The first discovered moon, it is simply called "the Moon"

COSMIC DATA: Earth's Moon is the fifth largest moon in the solar system and is the only moon to orbit planet Earth. Each year, the Moon moves about 1 inch farther from Earth. Earth's Moon is the only place other than Earth that humans have set foot on in space, and 24 people have visited the Moon—although only 12 people have actually walked on it.

PHOBOS

SIZE (diameter): 13.8 miles (22.2 km)

PLANET IT ORBITS: Mars (page 15)

DISCOVERED: 1877

NAMED FOR: Son of Ares in Greek mythology

COSMIC DATA: Discovered by Asaph Hall, Phobos is mostly made of rock. This moon is slowly moving closer to planet Mars—about 6 feet (1.8 m) every 100 years. At this rate, in about 50 million years Phobos will either hit Mars or break apart to form a ring.

Phobos is the larger of two moons that orbit Mars; the other—Deimos—can be seen to the right of Mars.

NASA has made recent discoveries that indicate there may be an underground liquid ocean on Callisto.

CALLISTO

SIZE (diameter): 2,985 miles (4,800 km)

PLANET IT ORBITS: Jupiter (page 16)

DISCOVERED: 1610

NAMED FOR: A nymph in Greek mythology

COSMIC DATA: Callisto is the third largest moon in our solar system—almost as large as the planet Mercury. Callisto was originally discovered by Galileo and was the first moon found to be orbiting a planet other than Earth. Callisto is one of the oldest and most cratered objects in the solar system and is estimated to be about 4 million years old.

Approximately the size of Earth's Moon, Europa has shown evidence of potentially having everything needed to support life; proving this will be the most critical element of the Europa Clipper's mission.

EUROPA

SIZE (diameter): 1,939.7 miles (3,121.6 km)

PLANET IT ORBITS: Jupiter (page 16)

DISCOVERED: 1610

NAMED FOR: A woman in Greek mythology (the continent Europe was also named for her)

COSMIC DATA: Europa is an icy moon with lines across its surface caused by breaks in the ice; these breaks are filled with a reddish-brown material. Scientists have been very interested in this material, and in the next few years, hope to directly study it with a new spacecraft called the *Europa Clipper*. It will take several years to get to its destination, but once the *Clipper*—equipped with cameras and radar—has reached Jupiter and begins orbiting, it will be able to study Europa with each "flyby".

IO

SIZE (diameter): 2,264 miles (3,643.2 km)

PLANET IT ORBITS: Jupiter (page 16)

DISCOVERED: 1610

NAMED FOR: A woman in Greek mythology

COSMIC DATA: Of all the objects in our solar system, Io has the most volcanic activity; there are estimated to be hundreds of volcanoes on this moon. Sometimes, the volcanoes are even powerful enough that they can be seen from Earth with large telescopes. This moon's orbit takes it through Jupiter's magnetic force, which gives Io its own electrical charge. Like Europa (page 31), Callisto (page 30), and Ganymede (page 76), Io was discovered by Galileo.

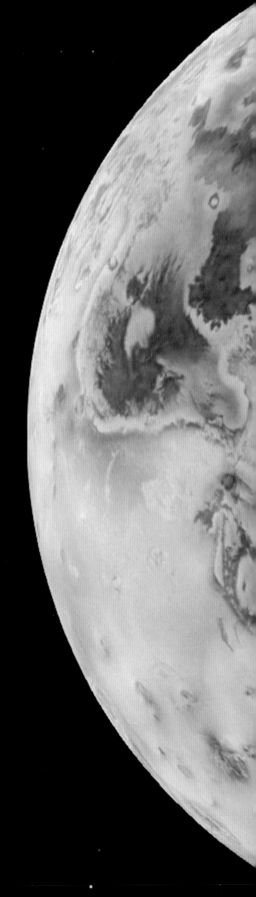

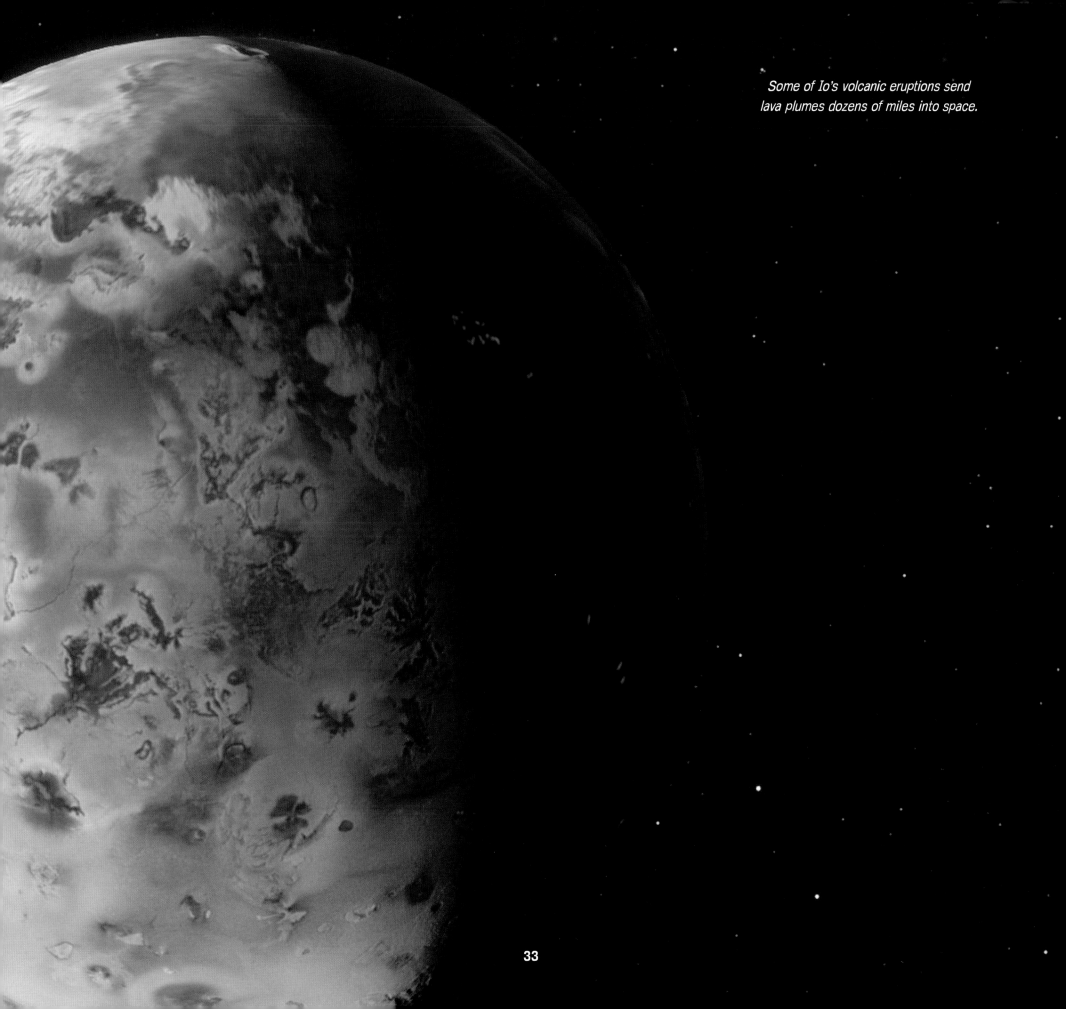

Some of Io's volcanic eruptions send lava plumes dozens of miles into space.

ENCELADUS

SIZE (diameter): 313 miles (504 km)

PLANET IT ORBITS: Saturn (page 19)

DISCOVERED: 1789

NAMED FOR: A giant in Greek mythology

COSMIC DATA: Enceladus is an icy moon that was discovered by William Herschel; the temperature on this moon is extremely cold at about −330 degrees Fahrenheit (−201 degrees Celsius). There is an ocean beneath its surface, and continuous eruptions spray liquid into space through cracks in the icy crust. Enceladus is Saturn's sixth largest moon, but it is still fairly small. For comparison, the planet is about as wide across as the U.S. state of Arizona. This moon's smooth, icy surface makes it the most reflective body in our solar system.

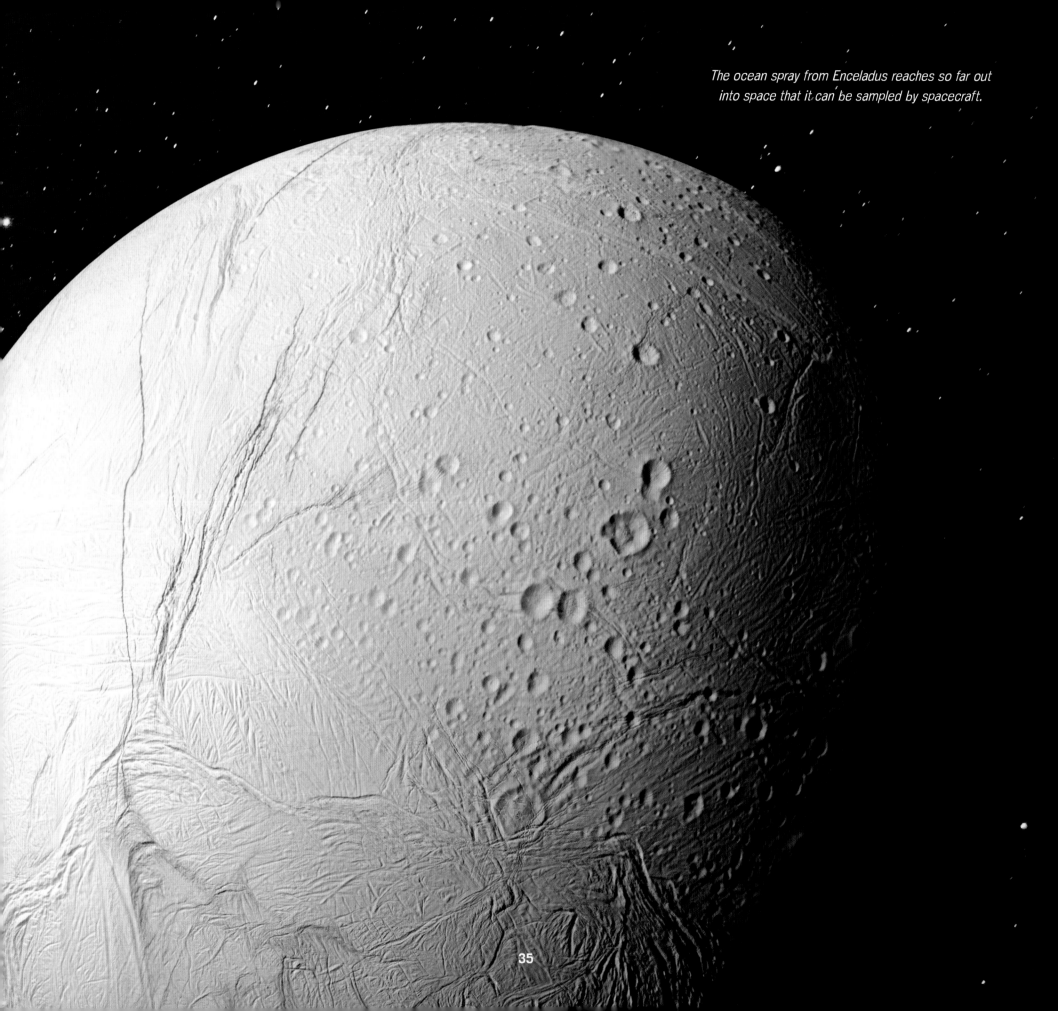

The ocean spray from Enceladus reaches so far out into space that it can be sampled by spacecraft.

RHEA

SIZE (diameter): 949.2 miles (1,527.6km)

PLANET IT ORBITS: Saturn (page 19)

DISCOVERED: 1672

NAMED FOR: A goddess in Greek mythology

COSMIC DATA: The spacecraft *Cassini*, named after the astronomer who discovered this moon, found evidence of a ring; this was the first time that a ring had been discovered around a moon. Scientists theorize that Rhea—the second largest of Saturn's moons—is made up of three quarters ice and one quarter rock.

DIONE

SIZE (diameter): 697.7 miles (1,122.8 km)

PLANET IT ORBITS: Saturn (page 19)

DISCOVERED: 1684

NAMED FOR: A goddess in Greek mythology

COSMIC DATA: Giovanni Cassini discovered this small moon. Scientists suspect that Dione is primarily made up of a dense core and ice. One of Saturn's rings sends ice powder (like smoke) onto Dione.

The Cassini spacecraft spent years studying Dione, and provided scientists with many images—including views of the long, winding canyons that cross this moon's surface.

OBERON

SIZE (diameter): 946.2 miles (1,522.8 km)

PLANET IT ORBITS: Uranus (page 21)

DISCOVERED: 1787

NAMED FOR: King of the fairies in Shakespeare's
A Midsummer Night's Dream

COSMIC DATA: Discovered by William Herschel,
Oberon is Uranus's second largest moon. Oberon is
made up of equal parts ice and rock; its surface has lots
of craters and at least one mountain.

TRITON

SIZE (diameter): 1,680 miles (2,700 km)

PLANET IT ORBITS: Neptune (page 22)

DISCOVERED: 1846

NAMED FOR: Son of Poseidon in Greek mythology

COSMIC DATA: Triton is the largest of Neptune's moons and was discovered by William Lassell just 17 days after the planet Neptune was discovered. Triton orbits Neptune in the opposite direction of Neptune's rotation, an unusual pattern called a retrograde orbit. Triton is one of the coldest objects in our solar system, with temperatures of −391 degrees Fahrenheit (−235 degrees Celsius), and an icy surface that reflects sunlight.

CHARON

SIZE (diameter): 753.1 miles (1,212 km)

PLANET IT ORBITS: Pluto (page 63)

DISCOVERED: 1978

NAMED FOR: A man in Greek mythology

COSMIC DATA: Charon orbits the dwarf planet Pluto and is about half its size. Charon has mostly been studied by photographs from spacecraft, which was how astronomer James Christy discovered this moon. Images show that Charon has a gray color to its surface.

Charon is dwarf planet Pluto's largest moon. NASA's New Horizons spacecraft has provided surprising images of canyons, mountains, and landslides on this moon's surface—which scientists had predicted to be covered in impact craters.

THE MILKY WAY

TYPE: Spiral

CONSTELLATION: Orion and Sagittarius

TRUE NAME: This galaxy has many names in many languages.

COSMIC DATA: The Milky Way Galaxy is of great interest to scientists because it is our home galaxy. Although it's hard to see something that our planet is actually inside of, on a clear night there are bands of light across the sky, which is our Earth view of the Milky Way. Our galaxy is estimated to be about 100,000 light years in size, and is surrounded by gas in the shape of a halo that makes it even larger. The Milky Way also has a large black hole at its center. If you could look at the Milky Way from above, it would look like it has a bar across the center. This bar is made up of gas and stars, and is the reason why the Milky Way's spiral is called a barred spiral. The Milky Way contains billions of stars, the most common type being the red dwarf star. Our solar system, including the Sun (page 53) and the major planets (pages 8-23), is located in the area of the Milky Way called the Orion Arm.

As of yet, scientists are not able to obtain actual images of the Milky Way from outside the galaxy...but by studying the parts that can be seen from Earth, as well as other galaxies, astronomers have been able to learn enough about the Milky Way to produce pictures of what it most likely looks like from space.

GALAXIES

Galaxies are structures in the universe where stars are formed. They are made up of dust, stars, and gas held together by gravity, and can contain objects like planets. Some galaxies have large black holes at their center.

There are three basic types of galaxies: spiral, elliptical, and irregular. Spiral galaxies are the most common, and have long arms coming out from the center that make a shape like a pinwheel. Elliptical galaxies are flat, smooth galaxies in the shape of an oval. Irregular galaxies are the least common type and include any galaxies that are not spirals or ovals; they typically have a blob-like shape.

Scientists don't know how many galaxies there are in the universe, but they estimate that there could be billions. Sometimes, galaxies get close enough to each other that they overlap, or even collide to form new galaxies.

Andromeda may be our neighbor, but even though it is the nearest galaxy to the Milky Way, it is still over two million light years away!

ANDROMEDA

TYPE: Spiral

CONSTELLATION: Andromeda

TRUE NAME: M31

COSMIC DATA: The Andromeda Galaxy is our nearest neighboring galaxy, and sometimes it's so close to us that we can see it on a clear night. It looks like a hazy patch or smudge in the sky. Scientists have been able to take pictures of this galaxy with the Hubble Space Telescope. In size, the Andromeda Galaxy is similar to the Milky Way. In fact, this galaxy is slowly moving closer to us, and scientists estimate that eventually the Milky Way and Andromeda will merge and create a new, combined galaxy. Don't worry, though. They don't think this will happen for another 4-6 billion years.

CENTAURUS A

TYPE: Elliptical

CONSTELLATION: Centaurus

TRUE NAME: NGC 5128

COSMIC DATA: Centaurus A is unusual because its shape is slightly warped, making it look like it has elements of a spiral galaxy. Scientists suspect that this active galaxy may be the result of a collision of two other galaxies millions of years ago. Centaurus A is about 11-12 million light years from Earth.

Centaurus A is an elliptical-type galaxy because of its long, flat oval shape.

THE SOMBRERO GALAXY

TYPE: Elliptical

CONSTELLATION: Virgo

TRUE NAME: M104

COSMIC DATA: Wondering how this galaxy got its name? The Hubble Space Telescope has taken pictures of the Sombrero Galaxy that show it has a long, flat shape with an unusually large bulge of stars near its center—giving it the appearance of a hat. Scientists think that the center of this galaxy may be a massive black hole. While not visible to the naked eye, the Sombrero Galaxy can be seen from Earth with the help of small telescopes at certain times of the year. It was first discovered in 1781.

THE WHIRLPOOL GALAXY

TYPE: Spiral

CONSTELLATION: Canes Venatici

TRUE NAME: M51

COSMIC DATA: Discovered in 1773, the Whirlpool Galaxy has since been photographed with the Hubble Space Telescope. This galaxy's well-defined arms are the source of its nickname. These arms are star formation zones; scientists think they may be so visible because a nearby galaxy has such a strong tidal force that it is causing more stars to form within the arms.

The Whirlpool Galaxy is a perfect example of a spiral-type galaxy because each of its arms are so clearly visible.

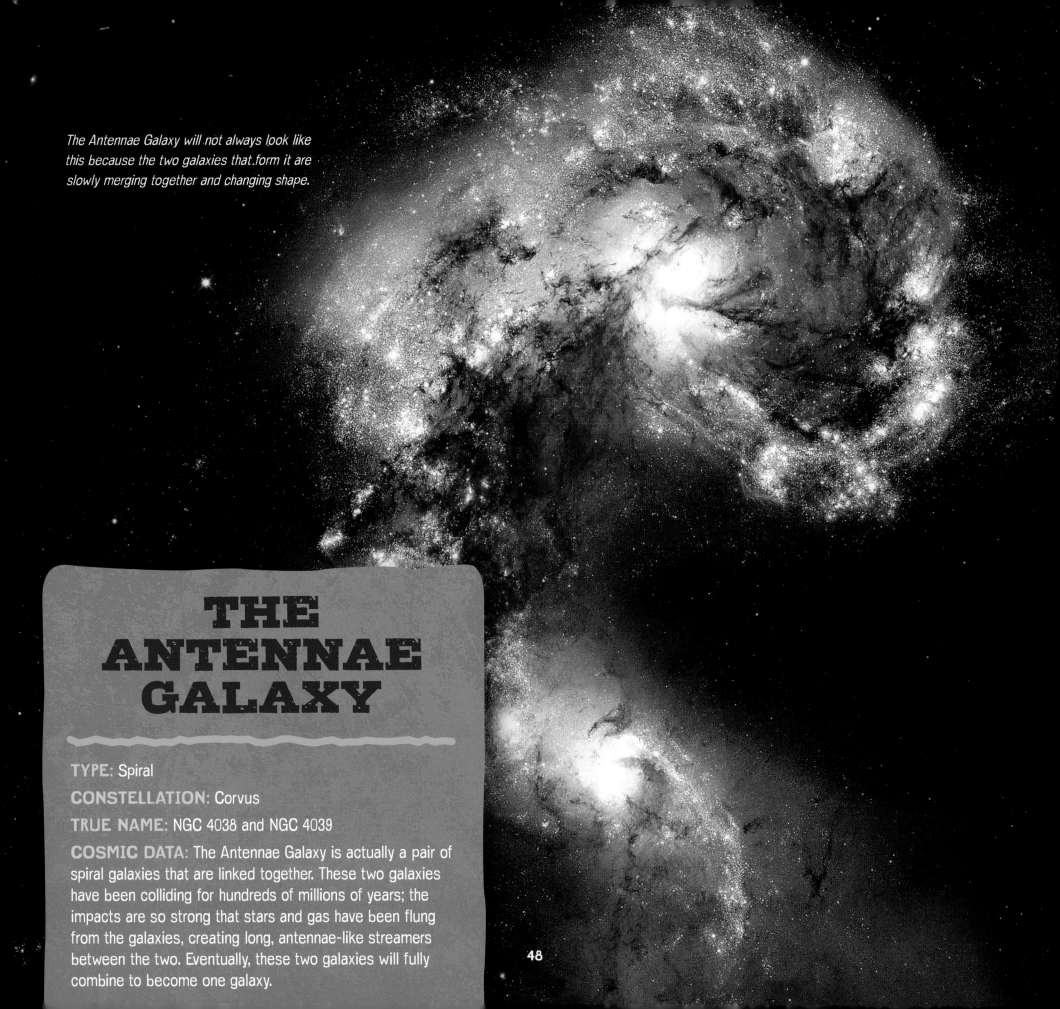

The Antennae Galaxy will not always look like this because the two galaxies that form it are slowly merging together and changing shape.

THE ANTENNAE GALAXY

TYPE: Spiral

CONSTELLATION: Corvus

TRUE NAME: NGC 4038 and NGC 4039

COSMIC DATA: The Antennae Galaxy is actually a pair of spiral galaxies that are linked together. These two galaxies have been colliding for hundreds of millions of years; the impacts are so strong that stars and gas have been flung from the galaxies, creating long, antennae-like streamers between the two. Eventually, these two galaxies will fully combine to become one galaxy.

48

THE PINWHEEL GALAXY

TYPE: Spiral

CONSTELLATION: Ursa Major

TRUE NAME: M101

COSMIC DATA: This galaxy's spiral arms are very well defined, thus giving it the appearance of a pinwheel. Scientists do not think that this galaxy has a black hole at its center, which is unusual. The Pinwheel Galaxy contains about 3,000 "starbirth" regions (star formation areas), which is the most of any observed galaxies of this type.

The arms of spiral galaxies are usually the regions where new stars are formed. Information from four NASA telescopes show that there are equal amounts of old and new stars in the Pinwheel's arms.

POLARIS

OTHER NAMES: Alpha Ursae Minoris, The North Star, The Pole Star, The Guiding Star

CONSTELLATION: Ursa Minor

COSMIC DATA: This star has been called the North Star because its location in the sky has allowed it to be used for navigation. Like Alpha Centauri (page 55), Polaris is actually three stars (a trinary star system); one main star has two smaller companion stars with it. It is possible that the North Star may not always be in the same location; Earth's axis moves over thousands of years, and eventually it might move enough to change where we see this star.

Polaris is at the very tip of the Ursa Minor constellation...better known as "The Little Dipper."

STARS

You might think of a star as a five-pointed yellow object, but stars are actually big balls of gas in the universe. While some stars can be yellow, they can also be red, orange, or blue. A star's color is related to its temperature. Cooler stars are orange or red, and the hottest stars are blue.

Stars have a life cycle. They are formed, or born, in giant gas clouds that heat up. The gas falls in on itself, and the star has its own force of gravity to keep that gas together in a ball. Reactions within the ball of gas cause the star to produce heat and light. Stars can shine for billions, or even trillions, of years, but they also eventually die. When a star runs out of fuel to keep it burning bright, it explodes and becomes a supernova.

The Sun is the center of our universe, and all of the major planets slowly rotate around it. Earth travels around the Sun in 365 days.

SUN

OTHER NAMES: The Sun is called many different things in different languages.

CONSTELLATION: None

COSMIC DATA: The Sun is a massive yellow dwarf star that sends light and heat into the universe. Unlike the other stars in this chapter, the Sun is visible during the day rather than at night. Without the Sun's energy, we could not have life on Earth. Light from the Sun travels to Earth in about 8 minutes. The Sun is about 109 times the size of Earth, and its core has a temperature of 27 million degrees Fahrenheit (15 million degrees Celsius). Scientists estimate that the Sun has only used up about half its energy, which means it could keep burning for another 5 billion years.

SIRIUS

OTHER NAMES: The Dog Star

CONSTELLATION: Canis Major

COSMIC DATA: Sirius appears in the sky as a single bright star, but it's actually two stars together in what's called a binary star system. Sirius A is the brighter of the two stars, and Sirius B is its smaller companion. This star system is actually slowly moving closer to Earth, and scientists expect that it will continue to do so for the next 50-60 thousand years. Don't worry, though. After that, they expect that it will slowly move away from us again. Sirius is also known as the Dog Star because it's the brightest star in the Canis Major, or Big Dog, constellation. The name Sirius actually comes from Ancient Greek, but it recently reappeared in pop culture thanks to the Harry Potter character, Sirius Black.

Like the North Star, Sirius has often been used for navigation because it is so bright.

ALPHA CENTAURI

OTHER NAMES: Rigel Kent, Toliman

CONSTELLATION: Centaurus

COSMIC DATA: This star is the third brightest in the night sky, but, like Polaris, it is actually three stars combined in a trinary star system, with one large star and two smaller companions. Mention of this star dates all the way back to English explorer Robert Hues in 1592. There is a planet around one of the Centauri stars, but it is so close to the star that it would be too hot to support life.

BETELGEUSE

OTHER NAMES: Alpha Orionis

CONSTELLATION: Orion

COSMIC DATA: Pronounced beetle-juice, this star was originally named for the Arabic phrase for "hand of Orion" because of the star's central location in the Orion constellation. Right now, this star is one of the largest and brightest in the night sky, but scientists suspect that it will one day die (or "go supernova"), and that the event will be visible from Earth.

Betelguese is a red supergiant star and can be found at Orion's shoulder.

This star is also referred to as "the heart of the scorpion" because it is the center of the Scorpius, or scorpion, constellation.

ANTARES

OTHER NAMES: Alpha Scorpii

CONSTELLATION: Scorpius

COSMIC DATA: This star is a red supergiant, and it is so large and bright that it was given the name Antares, or "rival to Mars." Scientists estimate that this star is 850 times larger than our Sun in diameter, and it is 550 million light years away from Earth. The star is estimated to be 12 million years old, and has been observed by people since ancient times, with mention of it going all the way back to the ancient Persians in 3000 BCE, where it was believed to be one of four guardian stars of the heavens.

PLEIADES

OTHER NAMES: The Seven Sisters

CONSTELLATION: Taurus

COSMIC DATA: This star is actually a cluster of several stars and is one of the closest star clusters to Earth. The seven largest stars in the cluster are the most visible, giving it the nickname The Seven Sisters, but there are over 1,000 confirmed stars in this cluster. Scientists estimate that the Pleiades is somewhere between 75 million and 150 million years old.

The name for this star cluster comes from Ancient Greece. In Greek mythology, the Pleiades were the seven daughters of Atlas, who supposedly held up the night sky.

This image of Pluto (page 63) was taken by NASA with the New Horizons spacecraft on July 14, 2015.

DWARF PLANETS

A dwarf planet is similar to a regular planet in structure, but it is too small to be considered a full planet. The difference between a planet and a dwarf planet can sometimes be hard to figure out—as we well know! Originally considered a full planet, Pluto was demoted to a dwarf planet in 2006, but as of 2017 that status is again being questioned.

The definition of a planet requires the object to orbit the Sun and have enough gravity to be round in shape. The biggest difference between a planet and a dwarf planet is that a full planet is able to clear its orbit path of other objects. Dwarf planets are so small that their gravity force is not strong enough to push away other planets.

Scientists suggest that there could be up to 200 dwarf planets in our solar system, many of which reside in an area called the Kuiper Belt.

PLUTO

DISTANCE FROM THE SUN: 3.7 billion miles (5.9 billion km)

SIZE (radius): 715 miles (1,151 km)

MOONS: 5

COSMIC DATA: Pluto is an icy planet; it has mountains covered in snow, but the snow is red in color. Pluto also has an intriguing surface—including a heart-shaped crater that's the size of U.S. states Texas and Oklahoma combined. One of Pluto's moons, Charon (page 40), is about half the size of Pluto, which is unusually large for a moon. Sometimes, Charon and Pluto are referred to as a double planet because of the moon's large size. Pluto was discovered in 1930 and was originally considered the ninth major planet in our solar system. After similar planets were discovered in the Kuiper Belt, this small planet was reclassified as a dwarf planet in 2006.

Pluto was named by Venetia Burney, an 11-year-old girl from England! Whether Pluto should be a full planet or a dwarf planet is still being debated by people all over the world.

The two moons that orbit this dwarf planet are named after Haumea's two daughters, Hi'iaka and Namaka.

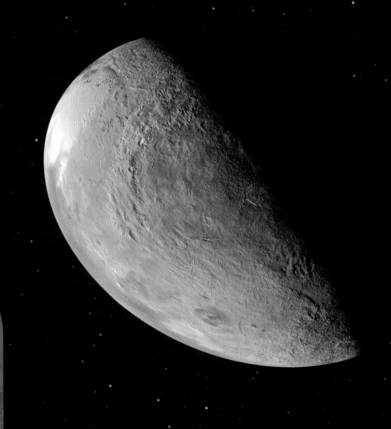

HAUMEA

DISTANCE FROM THE SUN: 4 billion miles (6 billion km)

SIZE (radius): 385 miles (620 km)

MOONS: 2

COSMIC DATA: Like Eris (page 66), not much is known about Haumea because of its distance from us, but scientists suspect that its surface is made of mostly rock and ice. Discovered in 2003, this dwarf planet is similar in size and location to Pluto (page 63). Haumea also resides in the Kuiper Belt, beyond the orbit of Neptune. This planet rotates so quickly that its shape is distorted, giving it a football-like appearance. It completes one full rotation in just four Earth hours. Haumea was named for the Hawaiian goddess of fertility, and its moons were named for her two daughters.

Scientists discovered a small object orbiting this planet in 2015, and suspect that it may be a moon.

MAKEMAKE

DISTANCE FROM THE SUN: 4.2 billion miles (6.8 billion km)

SIZE (radius): 444 miles (715 km)

MOONS: 0, 1 provisional

COSMIC DATA: Much like Eris (page 66) and Haumea (page 64), we don't know much about Makemake because it is so far away, but scientific observation suggests that, like Pluto (page 63), its surface is made up of ice and rock, and is a reddish-brown color. Makemake was discovered in 2005 in the Kuiper Belt, and was named for the Rapanui (Easter Island) god of fertility.

The discovery of Eris was what prompted scientists to first reconsider Pluto's title as a major planet, because the two objects are so similar.

ERIS

DISTANCE FROM THE SUN: 6.3 billion miles (10.1 billion km)

SIZE (radius): 722 miles (1,163 km)

MOONS: 1

COSMIC DATA: Scientists do not know much about Eris because it is so far away, but it most likely has a rocky surface and extremely cold temperatures like Pluto (page 63). Discovered in 2003, this planet is located in the Kuiper Belt, and was one of the first to bring up the question of planet versus dwarf planet. Eris was named for the ancient Greek goddess of discord and strife, and its moon is named for her daughter, Dysnomia.

66

What is the difference between dwarf planets and asteroids (page 83)? Dwarf planets are large enough to have a circular shape that is affected by gravity; asteroids differ because they are too small to form a sphere.

CERES

DISTANCE FROM THE SUN: 257 million miles (413 million km)

SIZE (radius): 296 miles (476 km)

MOONS: 0

COSMIC DATA: First discovered in 1801, this planet was originally called an asteroid, but since it is so much larger and different than other asteroids, it was reclassified as a dwarf planet in 2006. Ceres has a solid core and layers like a terrestrial planet, and some of the planet is even composed of water. This dwarf planet was also the first to be visited by a spacecraft when the *Dawn* reached it in 2015. Ceres was named for the Roman goddess of corn and harvests. Interestingly, the word "cereal" comes from the same name!

VOYAGER 1 & 2

MISSION: Exploration of Saturn and Jupiter

LAUNCHED: 1977

COSMIC DATA: These twin spacecraft have been making discoveries for more than 40 years. They were originally launched to explore Jupiter (page 16) and Saturn (page 19), where they made the exciting discovery of volcanoes on Io (page 32) and explored Saturn's rings. *Voyager 1* made history as the first spacecraft to reach interstellar space—which is what the area between stars is called. *Voyager 2* is the only spacecraft to have explored Uranus (page 21) and Neptune (page 22).

Both Voyagers were launched from Cape Canaveral in Florida, and both were so successful in their original missions that their explorations were extended.

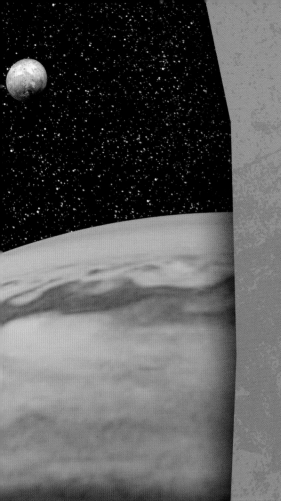

SPACE TECHNOLOGY

Outer space is so big and wide that it is impossible to see everything contained in it from Earth. Since the invention of the telescope in the early 1600s, scientists have been looking for new ways to explore space.

With the high-tech cameras and equipment that are now available, space technology has become very advanced. Some types of spacecraft just observe and monitor planets, while others can actually land and explore them. Today's space technology makes it possible for humans to travel to and live in outer space!

Two rovers were sent to Mars: Spirit and Opportunity. Spirit gathered data for six years, and Opportunity is still active today.

MARS ROVERS

MISSION: Exploration of Mars

LAUNCHED: 2003

COSMIC DATA: The Mars rovers were launched to explore the surface of Mars (page 15) to determine whether or not the planet ever had water on it. They both have mounted cameras and a robotic arm that works much like a human arm; these have allowed the rovers to take panoramic images of the planet, as well as samples of the planet's surface. You can even see where the rovers are now at: https://mars.nasa.gov/mer/mission.

Information from the Pathfinder mission suggests that at some point Mars was a warm planet with water sources.

MARS PATHFINDER

MISSION: Be the first robotic rover to land on Mars

LAUNCHED: 1996

COSMIC DATA: The *Mars Pathfinder* only explored Mars (page 15) for a few months, but it accomplished its mission of being the first rover to land on the planet; this paved the way for future exploration efforts—like the Mars rovers (page 70). The *Pathfinder* was equipped with instruments to study both the atmosphere and soil of the planet. This spacecraft had an innovative way of landing on the planet using technology that included a parachute and huge airbags.

Pioneer 10 and 11 were the first two spacecraft to ever leave our solar system; scientists do not know if the spacecraft are still transmitting signals.

PIONEER 10 & 11

MISSION: Exploration of Jupiter

LAUNCHED: 1973

COSMIC DATA: This pair of spacecraft far exceeded their mission to explore Jupiter (page 16) and were the first to reach the planet. *Pioneer 10* took images of the planet and collected scientific data on its atmosphere. *Pioneer 11* went past Jupiter and made the first observations of Saturn (page 19). Both missions have since ended when communications with both spacecraft were lost. The last signal from *Pioneer 10* came in 2003, and the last from *Pioneer 11* in 1995. Both will continue to float through outer space as ghost ships...until they are destroyed by a collision with a star or planet. A gold plaque was attached to each spacecraft; these plaques showed drawings of a man, a woman, and the symbol for the element hydrogen. If either of the *Pioneer* spacecraft happened to come into contact with other life forms, these drawings would be our message to them. The plaques are referred to as the *Pioneer* plaques.

The International Space Station has two bathrooms, five bedrooms, and a gym. It is as big as an entire football field...including the end zones!

INTERNATIONAL SPACE STATION

MISSION: Lab and home for astronauts in space

LAUNCHED: 1998

COSMIC DATA: The International Space Station is a livable space station created in a collaboration between 15 different nations and is the largest object humans have ever put in space. While construction on the space station wasn't finished until 2011, it has been continuously occupied since 2000. More than 230 people from 18 different countries have lived there, but it generally only has 3-6 people on it at a time. The International Space Station circles Earth every 90 minutes. You can track its location online (http://www.n2yo.com/), but it is also sometimes visible in the night sky—without a telescope—because the station is so reflective.

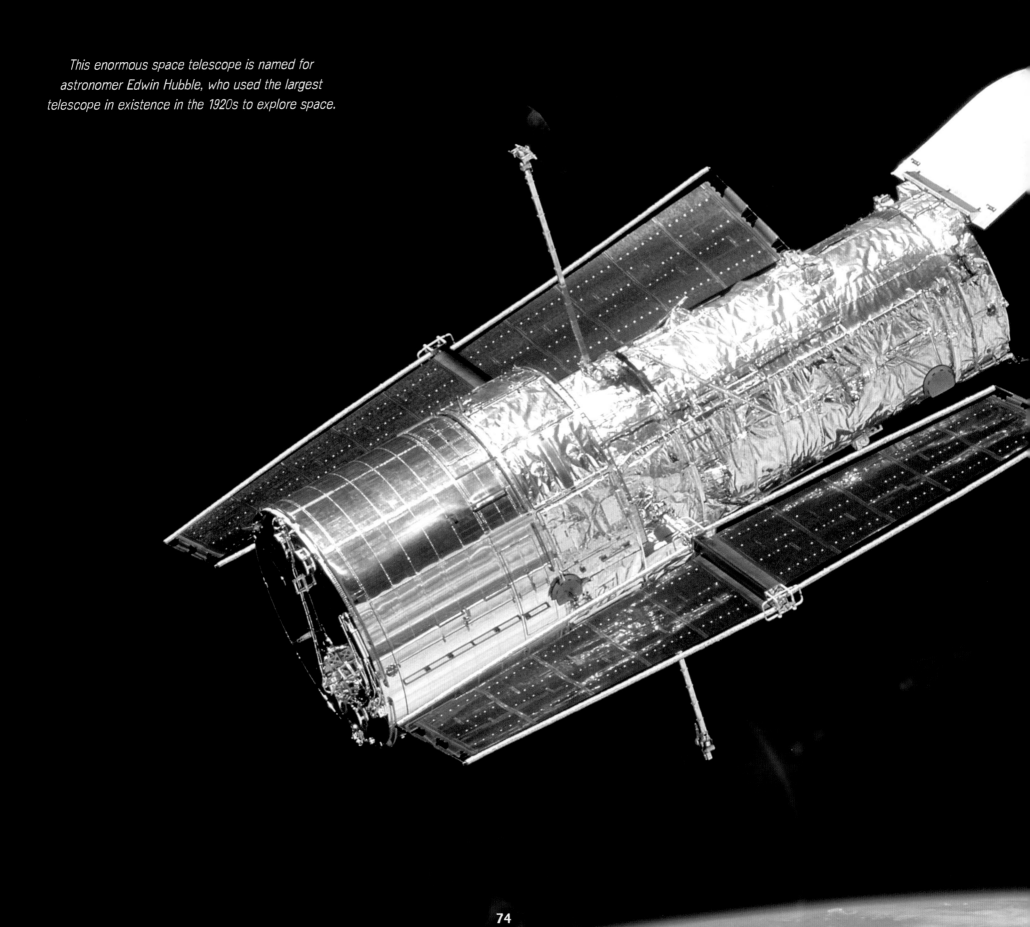

This enormous space telescope is named for astronomer Edwin Hubble, who used the largest telescope in existence in the 1920s to explore space.

THE HUBBLE TELESCOPE

MISSION: Observe space

LAUNCHED: 1990

COSMIC DATA: The Hubble Telescope was the first major telescope to be placed in space, and it has permanently changed our ability to view space. The telescope has been in operation since being launched, thanks to servicing missions to keep it functioning. The Hubble travels around Earth at 17,000 mph to take pictures of space and has made more than one million observations. The telescope itself is approximately the length of a school bus and weighs about 27,000 pounds.

Ganymede's icy outer layer is estimated to be 497 miles (800 km) thick.

GANYMEDE

SUPERLATIVE: Largest moon

SIZE (radius): 1,637 miles (2,634.5 km)

COSMIC DATA: This moon is so large that it rivals a planet, but it orbits Jupiter instead of the Sun. In fact, this moon is bigger than the planet Mercury (page 8). Ganymede has three layers: a core of iron, a rock shell, and a covering of ice. This moon was originally discovered in 1610 by Galileo and has since been photographed by the Hubble Telescope (page 75). Ganymede was named for a young boy in Greek mythology who became the cupbearer of the gods.

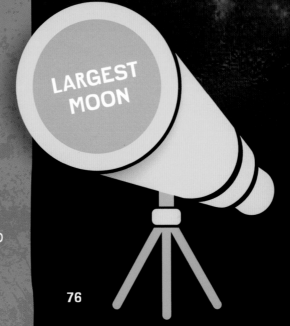

LARGEST MOON

SUPERLATIVES

The universe is made up of objects big and small, and each one is unique. Planets, moons, stars, asteroids, and meteors all vary in size and shape, and scientists have noted some particularly interesting discoveries.

Some of these unique space objects, like the Veil Nebula (page 80), Hoba meteorite (page 82), and star Deneb (page 79) can be seen from Earth. Space technology (page 69) has also allowed us to look at distant objects more closely and learn about what makes them special.

The universe is so vast that every object could be considered unique in some way, but these are a few of the most notable objects in outer space.

COMET MCNAUGHT

BIGGEST
COMET

SUPERLATIVE: Biggest comet

TAIL SIZE: 35 degrees long

COSMIC DATA: Comet McNaught—also known as "The Great Comet of 2007"—was spectacular in a variety of ways. Not only did it have an incredibly long tail, but it was also so bright that it was sometimes visible during the day. But what made this comet the biggest was not just its size, but also how it disturbed the space around it. The longer it takes spacecraft to get through the disturbed area, the bigger the comet's impact. The spacecraft *Ulysses* took 18 days to pass through the area disturbed by the comet. That's a long time! For comparison, the same spacecraft went through the wake of another large comet in just 2.5 days.

Comet McNaught, also known as C/2006 P1, was discovered by Robert H. McNaught on August 7, 2006. It was the brightest seen from Earth in decades.

Deneb is a blue supergiant, which means this star is hundreds of times larger (and much hotter!) than our Sun.

DENEB

SUPERLATIVE: Farthest visible star

CONSTELLATION: Cygnus

COSMIC DATA: Scientists estimate that the star Deneb could be anywhere from 2,000 to 7,000 light years away, but they aren't sure. What they do know is that, while the distance is incredibly far, Deneb is still visible in the night sky as part of the constellation Cygnus. Scientists think that this is the farthest star from Earth that can be seen in the night sky without the help of a telescope. The star's name is from the Arabic word for "tail and part of the phrase for "the hen's tail." Although the constellation Cygnus is now called The Swan, it also used to be thought of as a chicken.

FARTHEST VISIBLE STAR

THE VEIL NEBULA

SUPERLATIVE: Best-known supernova

EXPLODED: 8,000 years ago

COSMIC DATA: A supernova is what happens when a star dies out and explodes; the Veil Nebula is the wispy debris from one of these explosions. This nebula is so well-known not only for its delicate structure, but also because it is visible from Earth in the constellation Cygnus. The Hubble Telescope (page 75) was able to take images of this nebula, and scientists have estimated that the remains are of a star that was 20 times more massive than our Sun.

BEST-KNOWN SUPERNOVA

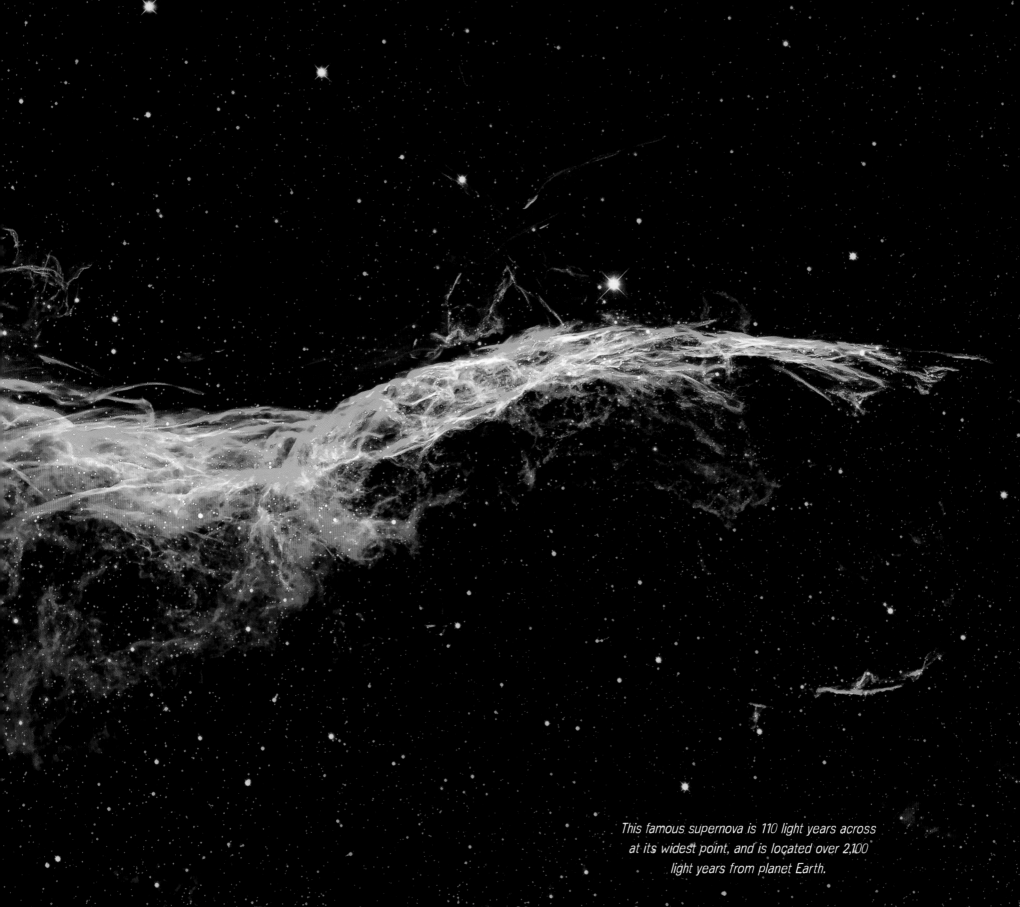

This famous supernova is 110 light years across at its widest point, and is located over 2,100 light years from planet Earth.

HOBA METEORITE

LARGEST METEORITE

SUPERLATIVE: Largest meteorite

SIZE: 9 feet (2.7 m)

COSMIC DATA: Chunks of meteors sometimes make their way through Earth's atmosphere and land on the ground as meteorites. Some meteorites are tiny—but sometimes they reach Earth as large chunks. The Hoba meteorite was discovered in 1920 by a farmer in Namibia and is the largest meteorite to hit Earth. The Hoba is made up of iron and nickel, and its weight is estimated to be about 60 tons. If you take a trip to Grootfontein, Namibia, you can even see this meteorite up close.

Because 71% of the Earth's surface is made up of water, many meteorites land in deep seawater.

Scientists used four separate telescopes to study this asteroid as it flew by Earth in October 2015.

2015 TC25

SUPERLATIVE: Smallest Asteroid

SIZE: 6 feet (2 m)

COSMIC DATA: Asteroids are any small, rocky objects orbiting the Sun, and they can range in size. The smallest ever studied is the 2015 TC25. This asteroid is a solid chunk of rock that, for an asteroid, spins incredibly fast—one rotation every two minutes. This asteroid flew by Earth in 2015, giving us the opportunity to study it. What also sets this asteroid apart is the lack of dirt or dust on it; because of this, TC25 has been nicknamed a "bald" asteroid.

SMALLEST ASTEROID

INDEX

A

2015 TC25, 83
Alpha Centauri, 55
Andromeda galaxy, 44
Antares, 57
Antennae galaxy, 48
asteroid, 67, 83
atmosphere, 5

B

barred spiral galaxy, 42
best-known supernova, 80
Betelguese, 56
biggest comet, 78
binary star system, 54
black hole, 5

C

Callisto, 30
Cassini spacecraft, 19, 36
Centaurus A galaxy, 45
Ceres, 67
Charon, 40, 63
Comet McNaught, 78

D

Dawn spacecraft, 67
Deimos, 15
Deneb, 77, 79
Dione, 37

E

Earth, 9, 12, 27
elliptical galaxy, 43
Enceladus, 34
Eris, 66
Europa Clipper spacecraft, 31
Europa, 31

F

farthest visible star, 79

G

Ganymede, 76
gas giant, 9
Great Red Spot, 16

H

Haumea, 64
Hoba meteorite, 77, 82
Hubble Space Telescope, 75

I

ice giant, 9
International Space Station, 5, 73
interstellar space, 68
Io, 32, 33
irregular galaxy, 43

J

Jupiter, 9, 16, 30, 31, 32, 68, 72, 76

K

Kuiper Belt, 61

L

largest meteorite, 82
largest moon, 76
light year, 5

M

Makemake, 65
Mars Pathfinder, 71
Mars rovers, 70
Mars, 9, 15, 28, 70, 71
Mercury, 8, 9
meteorite, 82
Milky Way, 42, 44
Moon, Earth's, 6, 25, 27

N

Neptune, 9, 22, 39, 68
North Star, 50

O

Oberon, 38

P

Phobos, 15, 28
Pinwheel galaxy, 49
Pioneer 10 spacecraft, 72
Pioneer 11 spacecraft, 72
Pleiades, 58
Pluto, 9, 40, 61, 63
Polaris, 50

R

retrograde orbit, 39
Rhea, 36

S

Saturn, 9, 19, 34, 36, 37, 68, 72
Sirius, 54
smallest asteroid, 83
solar system, 6, 42
Sombrero galaxy, 46
space, 5, 6
spiral galaxy, 43
starbirth region, 49
Sun, 5, 6, 53
supernova, 5, 51, 80

T

terrestrial planet, 9
trinary star system, 50, 55
Triton, 39

U

Ulysses spacecraft, 78
Uranus, 9, 21, 38, 68

V

Veil Nebula, 77, 80
Venus, 9, 10
Voyager 1 spacecraft, 68
Voyager 2 spacecraft, 21, 68

W

Whirlpool galaxy, 47

ABOUT THE AUTHOR

Boston-based writer and editor Kelly Gauthier loves stargazing and visiting the planetarium, when she's not reading. She is also the author of *Discovering Bugs* and *The Bug Handbook*.

ABOUT APPLESAUCE PRESS

Good ideas ripen with time. From seed to harvest, Applesauce Press crafts books with beautiful designs, creative formats, and kid-friendly information on a variety of fascinating topics. Like our parent company, Cider Mill Press Book Publishers, our press bears fruit twice a year, publishing a new crop of titles each spring and fall.

KENNEBUNKPORT, MAINE

Write to us at:

12 Spring Street

PO Box 454

Kennebunkport, ME 04046

Or visit us online:

cidermillpress.com